From Brick Buildings to Beaches

A MEMOIR

BY
SHARIKA K. FORDE

Watersprings
PUBLISHING

From Brick Buildings to Beaches
published by Watersprings Publishing, a division of
Watersprings Media House, LLC.
P.O. Box 1284
Olive Branch, MS 38654
www.waterspringsmedia.com
Contact publisher for bulk orders and permission requests.

Book References, © 2020 by Sharika K. Forde
The Awakening Book of Poems; Bare Emotions of Love, Growth and Self-Worth
The Awakening Book of Poems; I Dream in Color

Printed in the United States of America.

Library of Congress Control Number: 2021904121

ISBN-13: 978-1-948877-71-8

Table of Contents

Stage One: Sweet Dreams ... 1
    Childhood Memories ... 3
    Let The Games Begin ... 8
    Jersey Love ... 11

Stage Two: Escaping The Trap ... 15
    Florida Vacations ... 16
    Cookie vs. Marilyn ... 21
    Connecticut Living ... 24

Stage Three: When Puberty Strikes ... 29
    A Teenage Love ... 30
    High School Days ... 32
    The Decision ... 35

Stage Four: Primetime ... 39
    From Old Love to New Love ... 40
    Parenthood ... 43
    Mommy Dearest ... 45
    Fighting My Demons ... 47

Stage Five: Roller Coaster Ride ... 51
    To Have and To Hold ... 53
    Broken Vows ... 56
    Living the Single Life ... 59
    Finding Nino ... 61
    Let The Church Say Amen ... 64

Stage Six: Revealing Me ... 67
    Raising Boys to Men ... 69
    On My Own ... 74
    Back to Reality ... 76
    The Awakening ... 80

About The Author ... 85

Dedication

Although you are no longer here, I know you are watching over me.
This book is dedicated to my late grandmother, Anna B. Smith.

STAGE ONE
Sweet Dreams

Childhood Memories

My childhood memories begin around the age of five. I was riding my little training wheel bicycle back and forth in the kitchen, trying to run over every cockroach that dared to cross my path while my parent's voices, battling in the background, echoed throughout our tiny apartment. I was too young to understand what the argument was about, but even at a tender age, I knew that this was a regular occurrence in my household. Like many families, eventually, my parents separated. My two brothers and I became the product of a single-family household led by my mother. At least I wasn't alone in my sudden childhood confusion. Titus was the middle child, three years my elder. Titus and I would bicker over everything when we were younger. My brother Roman was ten years older than me. He used to call me Babygirl. When Titus and I would fight Roman always jumped in and defended me regardless if the fight was my fault or not. Being the youngest and the only girl had to come with some advantages.

There are parts of my early years with my mother and brothers that are a blur, but our many trips to the projects to visit my great aunt always stuck. I used to stare at the tall brick buildings as we approached the large metal doors to the entrance. The dudes rolling dice outside always had a dog by their side named King, a title we now crown our sons with. They cursed at each other over who won the last roll, yet would pause and clear a path so we could pass, their way of showing respect for women and children. As we entered the building, the pungent smell of the dimly lit halls, a combination of fried food, cigarettes, and urine, would capture your attention. Inside the two-bedroom unit, my mother sat for hours conversing, drinking, and laughing. My cousins and I passed the time by chasing each other throughout the dwelling. The sound of our rubber soles bouncing off the iron stairwell rang on every floor. My undeveloped mind not comprehending the grittiness of it all. For me it was a place we would go to visit family. It was Jersey.

Roman was my mother's twin. Tall, thin with dark skin, and very talkative. A Virgo, he had an opinion on everything and a story to go behind it. He took it as his duty to always keep a smile on my face and found ways to make me laugh even when he wasn't trying. At night, he would walk out of the bathroom with his entire face covered with Noxzema, and I would fall to the floor howling. The bright white cream against his dark tone skin was such a contrast. It resembled a Halloween mask. I was young, so skincare was not on my radar. Roman walked around the house with the silky paste on his face until it was so dry that he had to scrub it with a damp cloth to get it off. Although I found his nightly comedy routine hysterical, it also taught me that men cared about their appearances too.

At a young age, Roman lived the life of many grown men. Crime, drugs, and alcohol. He eventually became a product of his surroundings. Just one look at him and you could see the turmoil within as if a rain cloud hovered above his head everywhere he went. He struggled with addiction for many years. He went from being carefree and joyous to a person who was withdrawn and ashamed. But throughout all his ups and downs, he always found a way to keep in touch. The love he had for us, his family, remained clear.

My second brother, Titus, was three years older than me. Titus and I would bicker over everything; toys, television shows, and food. Thank goodness we were different genders, or I'm sure we would have fought over clothes too. I have to admit, I was purposely an annoying little sister.

Like most young boys, Titus was hyper, which made him accident-prone. One time he was in the kitchen boiling eggs and the container of salt was pushed to the back of the upper cabinet. He slowly placed his foot on the counter next to the pot to lift his body to reach the salt. On the way down, his knee tipped the pot handle. I stood there, stunned, as I watched the scalding hot water pour down his leg. The piercing scream that projected out of his mouth forced me to use my hands to cover my ears. The brown epidermis slowly pulled away from his body until the white layer of his skin was revealed. Scars he would carry for the rest of his life.

Titus's impulsiveness led him to another accident while he was playing a game of tag with a group of friends. One friend jumped off a two-story building and landed in the bushes below to get away from being caught. Remember when you were a little kid, and you wanted to follow behind your friend, and your mother would say, "If Tony jumped off a bridge, are you going to do it too?" Titus's answer would have been "yes". My brother followed after the boy in front of him without hesitation and jumped off the roof. Instead of landing in the bushes, he hit the concrete and shattered his ankle. The break was so bad the doctor's placed four metal pins through his leg to correct the bone damage. Titus was placed on bed rest and couldn't walk for eight months. I think the isolation he experienced was more painful than the fracture. As each month passed, he gained more and more weight. His body transformation led him to become soft-spoken, an attempt not to draw attention to his uncomfortable outer shell. It was during this time that he found solace in comic books. And what began as a distraction turned into an extensive collection that occupied the corner of his bedroom.

Memories of my brothers and I being home unattended in

our apartment in Rahway flood my mind. With Roman being so much older than us and living his own life, Titus became my caregiver as my mother would assign him to pick me up from my classroom every day and take care of me after school until she got home from work. Just another reason for his resentment toward me. One day when he was on little sister duty, he wanted to leave and go to the corner store and hang out with his friends. So, he decided it was time for a lesson in stranger danger. He warned me of the harm that would come if someone entered our home and snatched me away. After his lecture, Titus said he would be back soon and ordered me not to open the door for anyone. Before leaving, he glanced at me one last time as if he was contemplating whether he was doing the right thing. The door closed behind him, as his key turned, the click of the lock was his sound of security. I sat quietly in the middle of our living room, playing with my dolls. Seconds later, there was a knock at the door. Pushing a chair from our kitchen table to the door, I stood on top of it so I could glance out the peephole. I didn't see anyone, but then a voice exclaimed, "Hello, are your parent's home"? I knew it was my brother pretending to be someone else. Like I was instructed, I didn't respond. Titus walked away from the door, feeling comfortable leaving me alone. He was finally able to hang out with his friends after school. An hour passed and he returned home in one of the best moods I have ever seen him in. Later that evening, when my mother arrived home from work, the first thing that came out of my mouth was, "Titus left me by myself." The smile that graced his face soon faded as my mother reached for her belt to discipline him for not following her rules. Yup, I was the annoying little sister.

I was also a first-hand witness to my mother's 'Black Woman Fed Up Moment.' One day, out of the blue, my mother told Titus and me to pack some clothes in our book bags. We hopped in the car, assuming we were going to spend a couple of days at our aunt's house. Instead, my mother pulled into the driveway of a house I'd never seen before in East Orange, New Jersey. She placed the car in park and left the motor running as she ordered my brother and me to grab our bags and get out the vehicle. My mother walked us to the front porch. Her small hand pounded on the door with hard and rapid knocks. Before anyone answered, my mother,

My brothers on Easter Sunday.

turned around and scurried back in the driver's seat of her car. She shifted the gear into reverse and drove off. My brother and I were left staring at a door, not knowing who was on the other side. When the door finally opened, a woman stood before us, and a few feet behind her stood my father. He was playing house with another woman, and my mother decided to authenticate the experience by handing over his children. This was also the moment I learned my oldest brother Roman was not my father's biological son.

Let The Games Begin

Sylvia's buttery skin glowed as she opened the door with a welcoming smile. She had two daughters in their early teens, about Titus's age. Despite our sudden arrival, my father and his mistress attempted to build one big happy family. Titus seemed to adjust sooner than expected as he especially got along well with Sylvia's oldest daughter. I'm pretty sure my brother lost his virginity to our impending stepsister, as closets transformed into teen make-out spots. For him, our new living arrangement was heaven. Unfortunately for me, it was a living hell.

Since I was the youngest of the bunch and now a motherless daughter, I received extra attention from my dad and Sylvia. They showered me with toys and candy, and if cartoons were playing on TV, the entire household was watching them. Anything that distracted me from asking about my mother was granted. However, Sylvia's daughters were not thrilled about the special treatment I received. Even though it was their home, my father became king, the only other male in the house, Titus, was the prince and I was crowned little princess. Sylvia's daughters were tasked with taking care of me. If I needed a plate of food, a glass of juice, my shoes were tied in a knot, or my clothes needed to be ironed; the daughters were ordered by their mother to do it. It was Cinderella in reverse. But payback was a bitch. When no one was around, the sisters took their frustrations out on me, especially Sylvia's youngest daughter.

With three teenagers under one roof, the adults were able to go out often and enjoy their blossoming relationship. During those times, my brother would be entertained by the older sister in his newfound palace, while the younger sister took advantage of our home alone moments by getting revenge on the princess. My hair was thick and my standard two ponytail style became an easy target. While sitting quietly on the couch watching television, the younger sister would come from behind and yank my ponytails. That was minor compared to the multiple times I was spit on, slapped in the face, and teased for not having a mother. All by the hands of Sylvia's youngest daughter. I was never afraid to tell of the abuse. I would inform my father of every occurrence. He would question my brother about my accusations against the younger sister. My brother's fascination with the older sister kept him from being an eyewitness. Like most people who are confronted about their violent behavior, the younger daughter denied it, claimed it was an accident, or said I was exaggerating. Abuse comes in many forms and mine was in the shape of a jealous juvenile. Since I had no evidence, Sylvia's daughter went unpunished, and the attacks continued. Until one day, there was proof.

One morning all the kids were getting ready for school. Sylvia's oldest daughter was parting my hair down the middle for my standard style, while the youngest was burdened with making me a bowl of cereal. We were running late, and my father was rushing and telling me to hurry up and eat. I quickly dipped the spoon into the bowl and placed a large gulp of cereal in my mouth to speed up the process.

Immediately the taste of disgust consumed me, and I ran to the kitchen sink to spit out the revolting substance that filled my mouth. As my father looked at me with wonder, I exclaimed, "the cereal tastes funny." He opened the refrigerator door and removed the milk carton. We all watched as he slowly placed his nose over the opening of the container to conduct a smell test.

He then took a sip of the milk and concluded that it was perfectly fine. He became agitated with the thought of wasting food and yelled at me to hurry up and eat.

All eyes were on me as I consumed two small spoonfuls of cereal and almost gagged. My father walked toward me, unbuckling his belt strap, signaling that an ass-whooping would be next. In a firm voice, he ordered me to eat my cereal. I don't know if it was the look in my eyes or the expression on my face, but in that tense moment, he decided to put the belt down and taste the cereal for himself.

Jolted by the taste, he immediately spits it out and poured the entire bowl down the kitchen drain. Turning toward Sylvia's youngest daughter, he demanded to know what she put in my bowl. Terror took over her entire body as her 4'6" frame stood frozen in silence. Since she refused to speak, my father began his own investigation and started opening every cabinet door and drawer, searching for an answer. Finally, he looked in the bottom cabinet underneath the kitchen sink. As soon as he spotted it, he knew he found the source of the awful tang that filled his mouth, a bottle of Pine-Sol. While everyone was busy with the morning rush, Sylvia's daughter poured a house cleaner in my bowl of cereal. My father looked me straight in my eyes, and for the first time since being in that house, I knew that he knew that everything I told him was true. That was the last day I saw Sylvia and her daughters.

The younger me

Jersey Love

O ur next stop was Jersey City, New Jersey. My father found a third-floor three-bedroom apartment, which was perfect for our little family. I loved stuffed animals, and my bedroom was full of them. From bears to elephants to rabbits, if it was soft and cuddly, I had it. My room was my happy place, filled with everything I loved. I also loved this new place. Our street was lined from beginning to end with five-story brick buildings. More buildings meant more families, which meant more kids to play with. Saturday mornings were the best. My weekend routine consisted of turning the tv to PBS to watch Bob Ross. His pale skin and perfectly picked afro drew me in. I sat in front of the television mesmerized by how quickly he turned blank canvases into works of art, mixing one color with the next. From trees, clouds, mountains, and seas, right before my eyes the earth grew. After my weekly painting lesson, I would get dressed and play outside until the sun went down. Hopscotch, Red Light-Green Light, Tag, Hide'n'Seek; avoiding stepping on cracks or you will break your mother's back was all part of our playful competition.

During the short summer months, the temperature swelled, but you could always rely on one of the older boys on the block to get their hands on a wrench. All the kids would line-up in the middle of the street. Our clothes and shoes were soaked from the relief of the cool water sprouting from the fire hydrant that was illegally cracked open. Though our gratification was short-lived for soon after, the adults would begin yelling from their apartment windows, complaining because we drained all the water and there was nothing left for them to cook or bathe with. This was always followed by the wailing siren of the approaching fire truck, racing to shut down our makeshift waterfall.

The older girls organized a cheerleading squad, and our team went from block to block challenging other street squads. Each cheer seemed to begin with your name and zodiac sign, but it was up to each girl to come up with an ending line:

> *"My name Sharika and I'm a Sagittarius.*
> *I will blow your mind with my behind."*

Exclaimed with a twist in my hips, I had no idea what I was saying. All I knew was it rhymed. The guys played touch football or one of them would grab a milk crate and cut out the bottom with a knife and nail it to a wood light pole. Their homemade basketball hoop would entertain them for hours until the nails loosened and the crate landed in the middle of the street. Summer nights were comfy. I would walk by my father's room to say goodnight. He sat upright in his bed, watching tv and puffing on weed. Before I exited his room, he would request a kiss on the cheek, then wish me sweet dreams. Laying in my twin bed, snuggled with a soft, stuffed friend by my side; the rotating fan recycling the stale air, my eyes almost shut, and one flash away from dreamland until the jingle of the ice cream truck pleasantly disturbed my peace. Outside a swarm of children in their pajamas, mostly oversized t-shirts surrounded Mr. Softee for a late-night treat. As a child, I never understood why he drove down our street so late, but as I got older I realized his bell wasn't only an alert for children. He was selling more than just ice cream.

The winter months were cold and long, spent closed inside

playing Atari. Space Invaders was my jam. I sat still only with my fingers moving, trying to shoot every alien that fell my way. When the game glitched, you had to pull out the cassette and blow inside to remove the dust, then cross your fingers and hope that this simple solution worked. Most of the time it did. The first snowfall would bring all the kids back outside again. Back then, school closings due to inclement weather rarely occurred unless a massive storm was approaching. A day off from school signaled a silent alarm as all the kids would suddenly launch into a massive snowball fight. The large piles of snow left on the corner by the plow trucks became hiking mountains, as we quickly dash up the sides, trying to make it to the top. The majority of us would not be victorious in reaching the peak. But the slippery slide back to the bottom was just as rewarding. One Christmas, we took the train to the city to see the Rockefeller tree. The subway cars always made me nauseous, but the destination was always worth it. Whether it was spring, winter, summer, or fall, Jersey City was my playground.

Although children weren't the only ones discovering ways to connect, our parents had their share of adventure too. Now a single father, my dad, a handsome man whose thick mustache gave him a Billy Dee Williams vibe, was eyed by a lot of women in the area. But Cookie was the one that caught his interest. She lived on the fifth floor of our building. Cookie was petite, about 5'2" with bronze skin. Her S curl gave her shoulder-length hair the perfect wave. Her daughter Tammy and I were the same age, and we became close friends. Of course, I didn't know anything about relationships, but Cookie and my dad seemed to be a nice fit. They spent a lot of time together and my father entrusted her to guide me into becoming a young lady. Like the time we went to the department store so I could get fitted for my first training bra because, in Cookie's words, "I was starting to jiggle." She was fun, cute, and very easy to like. But competition was always waiting in the wings, especially for a single man taking care of his kids.

STAGE TWO

Escaping the Trap

Florida Vacations

My dad's side of the family was from the south, and most summers, we would spend a few weeks in Daytona, Florida, visiting my grandmother. My father's mother was a true southern woman. Grandma Anna was 5'5" with beautiful ebony skin and a salt and pepper Jheri curl. She lived on her own for many years and worked as a nursing assistant. The Baptist church was her second home, and she was a proud member of the choir. Sitting in the pews listening to her sing, you would have thought she was tone-deaf because her vocals were so off-key. But she belted out those hymns without a care in the world like she was Ms. Patti LaBelle. Between choir rehearsals and bible study, you could find her at church at least three to four times a week. On Sunday mornings, her 1982 white Toyota van turned into a shuttle bus as she offered to pick up anyone who needed a ride to church.

Even though it was our summer vacation, she would put us, kids, to work. We cleaned the house, washed and hung clothes on the line, cut the grass and watered the dozens of flowerpots that surrounded her one-story yellow brick house. Chores, she would normally do all on her own. She was the definition of a strong, independent black woman. Besides church, recycling also took up a lot of her time. You had better not dared to throw away a soda can in her presence. We had to stand on each one and crush it with our feet to prepare for the recycling bin. Her Toyota van had several uses and always came in handy for hauling her recyclables around town. It wasn't just her own soda cans and newspapers, she had numerous friends who saved items just for her. Upon our weekly visits, her friends would ask us inside for a drink of water or a glass of iced tea. I entered the house and tried to hide, however, their conversation always turned to me. Whose child is she? How old? She lives up north? Oh, she grew from last summer! On a few occasions, her friends would pull out a bag of "vintage" clothing that no one in the room could fit except me. Searching through the pile, they pulled out faded shirts and kulocks, then turned to me with excitement, exclaiming how good the items would look on me. To be polite, I pretended to like them. My luggage to return home would be stuffed with clothes that I would never wear. My father hated that.

My Grandma Anna.

Estrogen dominated my southern roots with a few testosterone cells sprinkled here and there. One summer, my dad sat me down and asked if I wanted to stay in Florida permanently, leaving my grandmother and aunts to raise me. Since I would soon be a teen, my dad could see that I was quickly blossoming into womanhood and needed a steady female influence around me. He was uncomfortable with addressing female issues. Like the time Titus and I were in the apartment in Jersey, and I received a package in the mail. Noticing that my name on the outside of the package was written in my father's distinct handwriting, I declared whatever was hiding inside was good. I teased my brother for not being the chosen child as I ripped the package open with enjoyment. To my surprise, planted inside was a box of Carefree sanitary pads accompanied by a pamphlet on monthly menstruation. This was my father's way of teaching me about the imminent changes to my body. My brother laughed uncontrollably. Needless to say, learning about my period was much more dramatic than actually getting it. I sometimes wondered what life would have been like if I said yes to staying in Florida. But I couldn't imagine leaving Jersey and being a bona fide daddy's girl, I declined.

Despite my decision to not live in Florida for good, I held a deep love for the Sunshine State, which was cultivated by the special bond between my cousin Gianna and me. Gianna lived with my grandmother, was a few years younger than me, and we were both December babies. We got along like sisters even though we only saw each other a few weeks out of the year. In Jersey, my brother, dad, and I only attended church on Easter, which meant my Sunday attire was limited to a few dresses. Without fail, every summer, I had to borrow dresses from Gianna, which she happily shared. My grandmother made sure to keep her busy by enrolling her in extracurricular activities. Gianna competed in swim meets, and even though I was a city girl and couldn't swim a lick, I loved watching her do her thing in the water. For her, swimming was as natural as walking was for me. She was a mermaid in the pool. Most competitions, Gianna was the only black girl contending, which made her easily stand out. When the whistle blew, she flew into beast mode and turned on her black girl magic, taking control of the pool. She was also in

My younger cousin and I.

a youth bowling league but eventually gave it up because her right arm became stronger than her left, which affected her true love, swimming. If you knew Gianna at a young age, you would clearly understand the unapologetic Black Goddess my cousin is today.

The Best family reunion was organized by Grandma Anna. Best was her maiden name. The reunion took place during Thanksgiving weekend, and each year it grew bigger and bigger. The gatherings brought together family members from all over the country, including Texas, New York, South Carolina, and Alabama. It was well organized with daily activities. Thursday was the traditional Thanksgiving dinner that was originally held at my grandmother's house, but our reunion got so large that it eventually had to be moved to the local community center. Friday was a free for all, usually a shopping day for those who wanted to take advantage of holiday sales. At night my aunt would gather like-minded relatives and spend the evening drinking,

My brother, my father, and I at Disney World.

smoking, and playing spades. Fish fry was always on Saturday, where I learned how to properly crack open and eat a whole crab. And of course, the weekend family reunion would end with going to church on Sunday.

My grandmother's house was a haven for our family. From her front door, a soft cool breeze encompassing the smell of the ocean would hit the tip of your nose. In just a brief distance, you could feel the cool sand melt in between your toes during early morning walks. Florida was where I received scars on my knees from learning how to ride a bike. It was the only place I had been where it rained on one side of the street and the other side stayed bone dry. It was where I developed my first crush, his nickname was Chu-Chu. His Jheri curl, slighted eyes, and cinnamon skin made him look like a younger version of Philip Michael Thomas from Miami Vice. We met at the family center, where they held programs for kids during the summer. Free lunch was provided and the day was filled with crafts and schoolyard games. During thunderstorms, my grandmother made us run around the house and unplug all of the electronics. She swore that lighting could go through the wiring and strike you dead. There was nothing to do but lay in bed until the storm was over, which meant you usually got a good nap that day. Playing in the garden was always a joy since I didn't have one in Jersey. We found an assortment of creatures crawling on the petals. Centipedes, beetles, and red ants were everywhere. And every now and then we would spot a tiny lizard in the grass. But my favorite was the ladybugs. We watched fireflies light up the sky at night then fell asleep to the sound of crickets chirping outside our bedroom window. Florida was chores, church, family, new friends, fish fries, and fun. Florida was the place that allowed me to connect eternally with my grandmother, cousins, aunts, and uncles. In one short plane ride, I went from brick buildings to beaches. It was priceless.

Cookie vs. Marilyn

O ne summer, my dad, brother, and I were packing for our annual trip to Florida. However, this trip included a surprise guest. Her name was Marilyn, a friend my father met at work. Her skin was golden and smooth like an expensive silk scarf. Her short curly hair complimented her plump cheeks. Her petite size didn't hide her coke bottle frame. We spent two weeks in Florida where Marilyn was introduced to our extended family. When we arrived back in Jersey, Cookie and her daughter Tammy saw us pull up to our building from their fifth-floor apartment window. My brother and I grabbed a few bags and trotted to the third floor. By the time we reached our apartment, Cookie and Tammy were standing at the door to welcome us back home. My brother and I went inside the apartment and Cookie asked about the whereabouts of my father.

I blurted out, "He's downstairs saying good-bye to Marilyn."

"Who's Marilyn?" Cookie asked.

"His friend that went to Florida with us," I replied.

My brother turned and looked at me. I shrugged my shoulders, confused by his glare. In one swift motion, Cookie transformed into an Olympic track star as my brother, Tammy, and I watched her dark curly hair fling back and forth as she flew by us and sprinted down three flights of stairs. By the time Cookie made it to the front of our building, Marilyn had pulled off, and my dad was on his way upstairs in the elevator. It didn't matter that

Cookie missed the opportunity to confront them face to face. The damage was done. Cookie made it clear that she was not going to be played. Even though she only lived two floors above us, as the months passed, we began seeing less of Cookie and more of Marilyn.

Marilyn and her adult daughter Marissa lived in a duplex across town from us. Marissa was the same age as my oldest brother Roman. Skin the color of honey, her 5'8" stature made you wonder if she should have been draped in designer clothes strutting the runway. Entering Marissa's bedroom, you were immediately struck by the bold red walls covering every inch. Besides the color, tacked against the wall next to the door was a Kamasutra poster displaying twelve zodiac positions. Sitting in her room, I would stare at the poster, intrigued by the explicit sexual images. There was something about Marissa that I admired. She was carefree and confident. The type of woman you couldn't help but notice when she entered the room.

My brother and I sitting outside our New Jersey house.

The more time we spent around Marilyn, I began to realize why my father chose Marilyn over Cookie. She pushed him into improvement. She was established in her career and owned her own house. Raising a daughter by herself for many years was a task that many women were faced with, but Marilyn made it look easy. She had goals and a plan for her life. Shortly after their courtship, my father purchased an investment property, a four-family home. Ownership was something my father always talked about, and he finally had the right influence behind him. It was time to prepare for another move. Purchasing his own home across town was a huge accomplishment for my father, but for me, it meant it was time to make new friends.

Petra and I clicked instantly. She lived across the street with her mother and younger brother. She was a jokester. To this day, I love being around people who can effortlessly make me laugh. You wouldn't see her without seeing me, and vice versa. We hung out at each other's houses every day after school. Then we would get the munchies and walk to the corner store and buy as much candy as the little bit of change in our pockets could afford. Sitting on our front stoops with our tiny brown paper bags filled with sweets, we watched the cars roll by and gossiped about the cutest boys on our block.

For two years, Petra was my ride-or-die bestie. Until once again, my father informed my brother and me that we would be moving. This time, the move was a big one. My father was offered an out-of-state job transfer, which meant relocating to Connecticut. The drug epidemic was hitting hard. Planes were allowed to cruise U.S. skies and dump kilos of crack in urban communities. The chemical warfare saturated the city. My father saw what happened to my oldest brother and wanted to ensure that Titus and I escaped what seemed to be the inner-city trap. This devastated me. I didn't know anything about Connecticut and wanted nothing to do with it. Of course, I didn't have a choice in the matter. This move was also different because Marilyn was joining us.

Connecticut Living

oving day came. Since Marilyn's furniture was superior to ours, we left most of our household belongings behind and packed up her place. Her daughter Marissa was taking over managing our four-family house and moved into our unit. One of the first things she did was paint, what used to be my father's bedroom, red. Everything was so hectic. However, I did manage to take a moment to say good-bye to my bestie. This was before the time of email and smartphones. Petra and I pulled out little pieces of paper, exchanged addresses, and promised to stay in touch with one another.

My eyes pierced out of the back-passenger window for the bulk of the two-and-a-half-hour drive. Static overcame the New York radio station blaring through the speakers, faded melodies indicating that we were distancing ourselves from the place I called home since birth and nearing closer to unknown territory. The landscape was covered with trees, grass, and single-family homes. It was calm in contrast to the streets of Jersey. Weirdly it reminded me of Florida. As we pulled off the highway, I gazed at a sign that read, "Welcome to the Town of Bloomfield."

Bloomfield was a small town, middle to upper class, and predominantly black. My father's job assisted him in finding a place for us to live. We turned down Talcottview Road and pulled into the driveway of a two-family duplex. The top exterior of the house was baby blue and the bottom half was white. My bedroom, the smallest of the three, was sandwiched in between my brothers' room and the master. My four-foot-high dresser housed my record player and 13-inch tv. That and my twin bed, nestled against the wall, were the only items that were sizable enough to fit in the tiny space. A couple of years later, I added an M.J. Bad poster to complete my preteen decor. This city girl finally had a backyard. Well, half a yard since it was a two-family house. Surveying my new surroundings, it was a completely different vibe from what I was accustomed to in Jersey. Talcottview Road, along with the next five blocks, were lined with identical two-family homes. The only thing distinguishing them apart was the outer color.

Our move took place in the middle of summer, but strangely no kids were playing outside. Sitting on the front steps, the sound of birds rattling the leaves in the tree from above my head was the only evidence of any existence. No kids were screaming from laughter. No cars were zooming down the street with pouncing music. No sirens screeching to get to the next emergency. The silence was eerie.

My dad decided to put the house in Jersey on the market and would drive back there every weekend to perform fixer-upper projects. I wanted out of boring Bloomfield so I became his helper. Although the only thing I did was hang out with Petra, still I made the trip back to Jersey with him every time. I became so familiar with the journey back and forth, that I knew how many McDonald's rest stops we needed to pass on route 91 before making it to our destination. On the way back to Bloomfield, my father always stopped at the last Mickey D's, and my standard order; a Big Mac, fries, and a strawberry shake, would be devoured before we made it back to the duplex. My milkshake was turned into a condiment as I dipped my French fries in it, a bonus treat. Summer was coming to an end, which meant my first year of school in Connecticut was about to begin. I wanted to look fly, so my dad took me shopping for new clothes at the Secaucus Shopping Center in New Jersey. Thinking back, we probably should have gone shopping in NY, but Secaucus was our regular spot. As a newbie, entering the 7th grade at Bloomfield Jr. High, I stood out like a sore thumb. To my surprise, most of the girls were cool and friendly. Inquisitive about my accent, there were a lot of questions about where I was from. For the boys of Bloomfield, it was a little different. I hit puberty when I was ten years old, which led me to be one of the few girls in seventh grade who had boobies. They looked at me as fresh meat.

I lived too close to school to qualify to ride the school bus. Along my daily walk, I met a girl named Sandra, who lived around the corner from me and would become my first friend in this new state. Sandra was a bit of a loner, but she had a great sense of humor. She was Jamaican, and her mom and stepdad were strict. They worked long hours. In their absence, Sandra was responsible for cooking, cleaning, and watching over her younger siblings. One Saturday morning, I knocked on her door and asked if she wanted to catch the city bus with me to West Farms Mall. Lingering around the mall or going to the movies were pretty much the only things to do. But Sandra said that she couldn't leave the house until she finished cleaning the bathroom. Because I was somewhat spoiled, my only responsibility outside of schoolwork was to keep my room neat, and that wasn't even fully enforced. So to me, cleaning the bathroom sounded like a cruel jailhouse punishment. I imagined her on her hands and knees with a toothbrush and bucket scrubbing each tile sparkling clean. I'm sure it wasn't that brutal. Although the expression on her face indicated that she wasn't going to the mall anytime soon.

Sandra seemed shy, but when she stepped outside of those confined walls, she became more herself, a sweet girl. But you could always tell that there was something deeper going on with her. There was a sadness that her smile could not hide.

By eighth grade, I had pretty much settled into the Bloomfield lifestyle and was eyeing a few boys. Bruce was the first one who caught my attention. He told his cousin Carla to tell me that he liked me. When she pointed him out to me, I thought he was cute, so I gave Carla my phone number to give to him. Bruce was popular. His reactionary persona labeled him a troublemaker by teachers. He was drawn to fighting and was good at it, so he never backed down from a brawl. Black pride also flowed through his tenacious veins. I heard a story once about Bruce sitting in the classroom, and the white girl sitting behind him called someone a nigger. Bruce instantly turned around and punched the girl in the eye. He was suspended from school for two weeks but said he would do it again with no hesitation. Bruce and I were the same age, but he stayed back one year, rendering him a grade behind me. He was the first boy I "talked" to, my first bad boy experience, and would become my first sexual encounter.

STAGE THREE
When Puberty Strikes

A Teenage Love

It was the summer before entering my freshman year of high school, and Bruce and I were still going strong, well, as strong as fourteen-year-olds could go. He called my house around 7 p.m., asking me to meet him at the corner of my street. The sun was setting, but I could see his silhouette standing by the light post as he watched my every step, inching closer toward him. Our eyes locked as we passionately embraced each other as if he were a shipwrecked sailor just returning home. We stood by the light post for what seemed like an eternity kissing and hugging, each refusing to release. This happened often. Our actions were fueled by a mutual physical attraction. We were teenagers. When puberty strikes, it's hard to hold back.

One day, Bruce called and asked me to meet him at the community center four blocks from my house. When I arrived, the only person there was a janitor sweeping the halls. Bruce pulled me into the ladies bathroom, and our kiss fest began. As we leaned against the wall, his arm extended to the light switch. Standing in complete darkness, his hand slowly moved down my back until he reached my knees. He applied soft pressure behind my knees and they instantly bent. Using his other arm to support my 100lb body, he gently laid me down on the bathroom floor. I was wearing a mint green jean skirt with a matching top, one of my fly outfits from Secaucus. Bruce moved his hand under my skirt and quickly pulled down my panties. A soft "no" escaped my lips, and I delicately brushed his hand away. In a tender voice, he replied, "everything will be ok". My mind and body surrendered. A single tear ran down my cheek as the unbearable pain felt between my legs rushed through my body. Minutes later, it was over. The bathroom was lit again. Covering my eyes with my hand to shield them from the bright light, Bruce reached his hand out to help me to my feet. As I stood, straightening my skirt, we both noticed a small pool of blood on the floor. The look of fear flashed across his face and Bruce immediately asked if I was ok. I was embarrassed by the blood and mumbled a simple "yea." He peeked out the bathroom door to see if anyone was in the hall, it was clear, and we exited the bathroom hand and hand. We parted ways outside of the community center with a kiss.

I rushed home as fast as I could as the blood was still flowing from my body. I reached my bedroom without anyone seeing me. Quickly changing, I threw my soiled clothes in the hamper and grabbed a Maxi pad from underneath the bathroom sink. I laid on my twin bed, playing the scenes repeatedly in my head. About an hour later, the house phone rang. It was Bruce, again, he asked if I was ok. I replied yes, then I apologized for getting my period. Through the phone, I could hear him trying to hold back his laughter as he informed me the blood had nothing to do with my monthly cycle. I went from feeling embarrassed to feeling stupid as a fourteen-year-old boy was educating me about my body. About a week after my encounter with Bruce, there was a knock at my bedroom door. Upon opening it, Marilyn was standing on the other side, holding my mint green skirt in her hand. While sorting the laundry, she noticed the bloodstain on the bottom of my skirt and questioned me about it. I lied and replied that I cut my leg and abruptly closed the door in her face. I never told a soul about the details of losing my virginity. That summer, Bruce and I continued to see each other, until shortly after I started high school. Since he was still at the Jr. High, our relationship naturally fizzled out. However, my time with Bruce wasn't quite over.

High School Days

The first couple of years of high school were pretty typical. I wasn't a studious child, but I did enough work to pass my classes. Lunch was the best, especially if beef patties or pizza was on the menu. The cafeteria was also a place where you could identify the divisions in the school. Even though Bloomfield was predominantly black, there were still cliques like any other high school. Athletes and cheerleaders in one area, high achievers in another. There was a table with girls from the boonies who shopped at Macy's, wore labels like Ralph Lauren, and carried designer handbags. The white kids and a handful of Asians were in one group. The Jamaicans with thick accents were in another. Then there were the kids who could blend in with any group like a chameleon. These kids didn't have anything that particularly stood out about them, but they also were not invisible. I was one of them.

By our sophomore year, Sandra's family decided to relocate to New York. I no longer had my friend from around the corner. But once again, I met someone during my trek home from school. Her name was Eunice, and although she lived in Bloomfield all of her life, at school she was sort of a newbie, transferring to the public high school from the local Catholic school. We initiated a conversation while walking home, and it was friendship at first sight. Eunice lived closer to the school than I did, in a three-bedroom Cape Cod-style house with her mom, younger brother, and stepfather. She was petite with caramel skin, relaxed, shoulder-length hair, a flat chest, a tiny waist, and a big round butt. She was a church girl so she wore a lot of dresses to school while the rest of us wore jeans, t-shirts, and Reeboks. The dresses she wore enabled her huge calves to always be on display, which she said developed from jumping Double Dutch. She also wore eyeglasses. Most girls with glasses were considered unattractive, but Eunice was different. Her round burgundy specs didn't hide her natural beauty.

Through our conversations, I learned that Eunice's family was from St. Lucia. I had no idea where that was. The only Caribbean islands I knew came from that commercial, *Aruba, Jamaica ooh I wanna take ya*. But one of the most impressive things I learned about Eunice was how rooted she was in her faith. Don't get me wrong she was interested in all the normal teenage girl subjects, boys, clothes, and music. Her favorite R&B singer was Bobby Brown, and we all know how provocative he was. However, she didn't let those things jeopardize her morals. Believe it or not, throughout our high school years, I teased her about being a virgin. I didn't understand the point in saving your virginity. My immature mind thought that if you were in a relationship with someone, sex was something you were supposed to do. Eunice had plenty of suitors in high school. None had popped her cherry.

Meanwhile, things between Marilyn and my dad were getting so bad that they decided to split. Instead of returning to Jersey, Marissa, Marilyn's daughter, moved to Connecticut, and they shared a townhouse in Windsor, the neighboring town. I had no emotions about the dissolution of their relationship. Due to my stubborn ways, Marilyn and I never connected. To this day, I still have issues with truly letting women into my life. I'm sure Iyana Vanzant has a psychological term for daughters raised without their biological mothers. I can picture myself sitting next to her on the couch, finally reaching a breakthrough and crying uncontrollably into her large breasts, as Iyana rocks me back and forth, rubbing my back and calling me "Beloved." With Marilyn now off on her own, our little family was back to three. Then another change occurred, another move, but this one was only a short distance. My dad secured a townhouse in the center of Bloomfield with a tennis court, playground, and pool. I really should have taken swimming lessons when I was in Florida.

After our move, my oldest brother Roman showed up, at our door, out of the blue. The last time I saw him, back in Jersey, he brought home a King Tut statue that he made in Job Corps. He painted it gold, blue, green, and red. Roman was so proud of that statue. This beautiful piece of art was something he created with his own two hands. After the statue fell off the coffee table and the snake broke off of King Tut's head, holding it in his hands still gave him so much gratification. My oldest brother, my childhood protector, had been wrestling his demons for years. My father persuaded him to move to Connecticut to get a fresh start.

The Decision

T hings took a dramatic shift during my junior year of high school. Although Bruce and I hadn't "talked" to each other for a few years, we were still in touch. In between classes, we would pass one another in the halls and parade a wink or a slight smile to catch each other's attention. There was still an attraction. Occasionally we would go beyond minor flirting in the halls. The truth was, I was more than just attracted to Bruce. He was my first love. Even though a few years had passed, my feelings for him hadn't disappeared. Our minor flirting turned into casual hookups. And before I knew it, my life turned into an episode of *16 and Pregnant*.

The thought of becoming a mother at such a young age gave me mixed feelings. On one hand, I was afraid. How was I going to take care of a child when I could barely tend to myself? On the other hand, I wanted it. I wanted something to love that would unconditionally love me back. Bruce, however, was clear on his decision. He flat out told me that if I had the baby, he would have nothing to do with it. He used our age to rationalize his preference and vigorously stated that it would ruin both of our lives. But the hardest part of all of this was breaking the news to my father. I was his little girl, his princess. My father arrived home from work one evening, and I sat him down to have the talk. I can't remember the exact words I said. I do remember his anger afterward. My father ordered me to pick up the phone and call Bruce's house so he could speak to his parents. Somehow in this bleak moment in my life, I found the courage to refuse my father's request. With every harsh word Bruce said to me, I was still protecting him. Ultimately, the decision was made that I was not going to bring a child into the world.

A few days later, I found myself sitting in a waiting room clinic. When the nurse called my name, my father stood up to accompany me. The nurse motioned him to sit down, and I followed behind her by myself as the door quietly shut behind me. As we walked toward the room, I was already imagining that dreadful table with the stirrups at the end. To my surprise, the room we entered housed two chairs and a small table covered with pamphlets. The woman was a social worker and she wanted to talk before the procedure. We sat across from each other as she introduced herself. Holding a clipboard, she proceeded to ask me a few questions. My age, the age of the father of the baby, who lived in my household, what grade I was in; etc. Then she reviewed all of my options, and the resources available for assistance. Finally, she asked if I wanted to continue with the procedure. That question triggered my mind to rewind and I heard everything my father and Bruce said to me. In my hesitation, I looked up at the woman. As our eyes met, she spoke in a soft comforting tone and said, "it's your choice."

There was finally someone who cared about how I felt. At that moment, I found my voice and I said "No." The social worker handed me her business card and a handful of pamphlets as she walked me back to the waiting room to confront my father. It was my turn to sit and wait as the social worker spoke to him behind closed doors. After a few minutes, the door swung open, and I followed behind my father as he swiftly exited the clinic. However, my escape was temporary. A week later, I found myself back at the clinic, this time making it into the room with the dreadful stirrup table. Returning to school after taking a week off to heal, I fell right back into my teenage routine as if the whole thing never happened. From time to time, I would think back and ask myself, "what if?" One thing I was certain about was that my relationship with Bruce was over.

The seed that grew inside of me, changed my life completely.
I turned to you for support but you destroyed all my hope.
We laid together and made a baby, then you deserted me.
The sex, you couldn't resist but claiming too young to handle this.
Turning to my father for one last hope. His eyes spoke his words.
The decision wasn't mine to make. It ended in one day.
Stolen away through abortion. I hated you for not supporting me.
Years later I still feel the pain. My first child had no name.

STAGE FOUR
Primetime

From Old Love to New Love

I was seventeen and nearing the end of my junior year of high school when Edwin walked into my life. Edwin was dark-skinned, 5'10" with a slim build, and spoke with a modest West Indian accent. His family moved from Barbados to the States when he was an adolescent. One day when I was walking home from getting some snacks from the convenience store, I passed a group of guys playing basketball. I was walking on the opposite side of the street from where they were playing, and Edwin ran across the road and stopped me in my tracks. He was charming. I gave him my number and we spoke over the phone that night.

Edwin was out of high school and five years my senior. If he were to tell the story, he would say that I lied to him about my age. I did not. This was my first time dating an older man. We went on a few dates, usually dinner and a movie, but instantly I knew he had a kind heart. He introduced me to his close friends, his five sisters, and his father. His mom and two brothers still resided in Barbados at the time. He was a huge Tupac fan, which eventually made me one too. He worked two jobs. A school bus driver during the day, and McDonald's cook at night. He shared a place with his older sister, close to the subsidized housing units they grew up in. Edwin and I spent as much time together as humanly possible. Within a short period I became smitten.

Although I was in a new relationship, my heart wasn't healed from the wound left behind from my pregnancy. Deciding to terminate it left an emptiness inside of me. Since Edwin was much older, he was in a different headspace than boys my age. After a few months of romancing, I became pregnant again, but this time it was on purpose. Purposely planning to get pregnant at seventeen sounds preposterous. But in our minds, we thought we could handle it. The baggy clothing style of the '90s did a good job of concealing my growing belly, and by the time my father found out, I was toward the end of my second trimester. I couldn't muster up the courage to tell him about my pregnancy right away. I was too afraid of disappointing him again. He walked into my room one day and stumbled upon a medicine container left on top of my dresser. It was my prenatal vitamins. After my father found out that his teenage daughter was pregnant for a second time, he became so upset that he completely stopped speaking to me. He spent most of his nights at a girlfriend's house, still living under the same roof with someone who doesn't want anything to do with you was unpleasant, to say the least. Regardless, I didn't let that stop me from preparing for my baby. Edwin had a JCPenney credit card and we maxed it out on a baby shopping spree. We decided to wait to find out the gender, so my teen-girl, pale pink bedroom quickly converted into a sage green and yellow nursery. A white crib and mattress were in the corner and I had a stockpile of diapers, wipes, baby powder, shampoo, and neutral-colored clothing. Mostly onesies and pajamas. I felt like we were ready.

The contractions began one winter night while I was home alone watching television. The pain pulsated from my pelvis to the top of my round protruding belly. It was the worst pain I felt in my life. Edwin, still working as a school bus driver, picked up extra hours by transporting one of the local high school basketball teams to their game, which was forty-five minutes away. I paged him 911. He found a payphone nearby and called me back immediately. It was a week before my due date, but I knew it was time. Edwin said the game was almost over, and he would be at my house as fast as he could. I called my bestie Eunice who was also on baby watch. She borrowed her mother's Ford Escort and drove to my house. My contractions were minutes apart, but I refused to leave without Edwin by my side. I was in agony by the time he arrived. Edwin helped me into the passenger seat of his car as Eunice trailed behind us as we rushed to Mt. Sinai hospital. I was promptly admitted. The nurse led me to the bathroom to change into a gown, and a burst of liquid fell from between my legs and splattered on the floor. My water broke. The nurses hurried me into the delivery room. Edwin was standing by my side, holding my hand, and I could see Eunice, in the shadows, standing in the corner of the room. On December 19, 1991, twelve days after my eightieth birthday, my first son entered the world.

My first son.

Parenthood

He was beautiful. Skin the color of brown sugar, the soft curly hair only occupying the top of his head, made him look like he was born with a haircut. His arched eyebrows perfectly frames his bright eyes. He was everything I imagined. I counted every little finger and toe to make sure they were all there. I was no longer just a teenager, no longer just a high school senior. I was someone's mother, and I was instantly in love. After spending two days in the hospital, I was sent home with a newborn to take care of. Just over 7lbs and 19 inches long, besides feeding and changing diapers, neither Edwin nor I had any idea how to raise a child. All of our preparation had mainly been for our son's materialistic needs. What we did not consider was how parenthood would change us emotionally.

The first few months of being first time parents were rough. Edwin was still working two jobs, and I was trying to balance my schoolwork and being a new mother. On top of that, my mental state was all over the place. There were moments when I felt like I was the best mom in the world, like when he burped right after a bottle, or how calm he was when I gave him a warm bath, or when he slept for three hours straight. But then there were times that I felt like a failure. When there was random non-stop crying, and the only thing that seemed to settle him down was a ride in the car. My plan to breastfeed turned out to be a disaster. After a month, my nipples became so raw it was too painful to continue nursing. Thank goodness for Edwin's sister who told us about WIC. The expense of paying for baby formula was not part of our plan. And between the diaper rashes, cradle cap, and the mysterious little red bumps that formed on his cheeks, I wasn't sure if I should lay him in the crib naked to let his skin heal naturally, or cover him in ointments and creams. Oh, and all the advice you receive as a new parent is another thing. When you are a first-time parent, every woman who has ever given birth is waiting for the opportunity to instruct you on what to do. Everyone's advice is different. Needless to say, we got through it, but the majority of my frustration was taking out on Edwin.

Besides the pressure of being a mother and finishing high school, I was also one-half of a relationship. What Edwin and I thought would be an easy road for us to tackle, turned into our biggest test. Only dating for a short time before I became pregnant, my focus turned from Edwin to the baby even before he was born. In striving to be the best mother I could, I neglected the one person who helped to bring my little bundle of joy into the world. Edwin and I began arguing over everything. In a matter of months after giving birth, my fantasy romance began to turn into a nightmare. I managed to graduate on time and walk

the stage with the rest of my senior class. But my relationship with Edwin was on bumpy ground.

High School graduation.

Mommy Dearest

The summer after I graduated from high school, my father announced another move, this time to the state of Maryland. He invited the baby and me to join him. Although things were not good with my relationship with Edwin, he was a good father, and I didn't want to move our son away from him, so I stayed in Connecticut. My brother Titus had his own place by then, and Roman had returned to New Jersey. My father rented a one-bedroom apartment for me and the baby in East Windsor, a few towns over. One night, after my dad moved out of state, I received a phone call from him. He said that he received news that my mother passed away. After we moved to Connecticut, my communication with her was limited. She called Titus and me from time to time to see how we were doing. The last time I spoke to her was after Roman told her I was having a baby. She was extremely upset at the shocking news. I was already fully aware of how disappointed my father was in the choices I made, and I was in no mood to hear that I was also a failure to my mother. A woman who I considered a stranger. The conversation began with her asking me if my pregnancy was true. I proudly exclaimed, "Yes." The boldness in my voice angered her even more as she began to bash my father's parenting skills. She said he never wanted me. She continued saying that when my father found out that she was pregnant with me that he told her to get rid of it, but she refused. I was briefly speechless. Knowing that she knew nothing about the termination of my first pregnancy, I found that she wasn't just throwing jabs, instead, she was speaking the truth. Regardless, I responded, vehemently defending my dad. I said, "It doesn't matter if he didn't want me because he took the time to raise me, which is something you never did." Then I slammed the phone down and hung up. That was the last conversation I had with my mother before her death.

With my baby in tow, Titus and I rode the train to New Jersey and met our father at the station. My mother was only in her late forties when she passed away. I was told the cause of death was heart failure, but I also knew, like Roman, that she had a history of substance abuse. Roman was a complete wreck. He had lost his best friend. The one person who was always there for him. We walked into the closed casket service. The room was small but big enough to house immediate family and close friends. Following the service, I waited in the limo with my son, shortly after, Titus entered the limo, wiping tears from his eyes. The opposite of his stoic behavior during the service. I knew something transpired in my absence. Me being the annoying little sister, questioned him until I finally got an answer. He said, "they opened the casket." While I was waiting in the limo with the baby, the family held my two brothers back so they could see my mother one last time. My mind went from motherless child to furious daughter. Why wasn't I given the option to see her? I found out it was my father's decision. He didn't think his eighteen-year-old daughter could handle looking at death even though I had recently given life. Afterward, the family gathered at my uncle's house. Even though we only lived a few hours apart, this was the first time I had been around my Jersey family since I was a little girl. We made a promise to reunite at least once a year. However, it never came to fruition. Up to this day, I have never shed tears over my mother's death.

Fighting My Demons

ast forward a few years, Edwin and I were working hard to make our relationship strong. Regardless of our love dance, an on-again-off-again romance, we continued to build our family, and I had given birth to our second son. Depression hit me but managing through life seemed to be my specialty. No one ever knew what I was going through, because I refused to let it show on the outside. I constantly pondered whether Edwin loved me. Or if he was with me just because of the kids. My fear of becoming another teen mom statistic, having multiple babies, and living in poverty, was something I thought about often. In my mind, I had to make sure that I proved all the doubters wrong. I placed pressure on myself that wasn't there, all due to fear of how I would be judged. There were times when the pressure mounted, and I couldn't hold it in any longer. After an argument with Edwin, I ran to the bathroom and grabbed a bottle of Tylenol. It was the strongest thing we had. I swallowed half the bottle then laid in my bed and waited. Thirty minutes passed and all I attained was a massive stomachache. I got up from the bed and walked downstairs. As I passed Edwin who was sitting on the couch, he suspiciously watched me enter the kitchen. With a knife hidden inside my shirt sleeve, I swiftly went back to the bedroom. Sitting inside our bedroom closet, the only place I could find to hide, I wept heavily at the thoughts I was contemplating. The cries rang throughout the house as Edwin made his way upstairs to check on me. When he opened the closet door, I was bleeding from my wrist. He yelled, "Are you crazy?" Then, he carried me into the bathroom to examine the damage. The cut wasn't deep. It just pierced the skin.

Sometimes I wish I were dead, maybe then you'll be happy.
At least I won't be the blame for this catastrophe.
Maybe then you can enjoy the things that we gained.
Without me here creating any pain.
But the cut wasn't deep enough, it just broke the skin.
Next time I'll cut deeper. It'll work then.
Then I will be laid to rest from all these years of neglect.
Then you will realize the pain I felt.
My feelings for you were true. I loved you with all my heart.
Maybe dying is the only thing that can break us apart.
Tell my children I love them, but my life wasn't meant to be.
Make sure they know that they were not the cause of my misery..
To you, I want to say, I am sorry for all the pain.
I really thought love could conquer everything.
To my family, I'll miss you, but please don't cry.
This was something I wanted, I just wanted to die.

But I didn't want to die. I wasn't ready for my life to end. Truth was, I was lost. It wasn't only postpartum. Throughout my life, I dealt with moments of depression. I always felt alone, even when people were surrounding me. After my suicidal episode, I found a new way to fight my mental demons that were less noticeable. I took it out on my hair. Hair is the one thing that most of us have control of. We can color it, straighten it, or curl it. I spent years growing my hair out. I always strived for shoulder length. I would reach my optimal goal. My strands were healthy and long. Then out of the blue, I would go to the salon and request for it to be chopped off in a short Toni Braxton do. This happened multiple times in my young adult life. Internally, I was in constant motion spinning in every direction. My hair was the one thing I had control of. Legally, I was an adult but sometimes my mind would rewind to a lost little girl, and I cut my hair off every time. See, I understood when Britney Spears grabbed those scissors and cut off her golden locks. She was lost and decided to take back her control in front of the entire world.

Despite my mental state, I pushed on with my daily routine as if everything was okay. Months passed, and life was actually going pretty well, and my relationship with Edwin improved. One morning I was carrying a laundry basket full of clothes, and I suddenly felt faint. I called out to Edwin right before I collapsed to the floor. Edwin heard the loud thump and ran to me. He shook my body. My eyes rolled to the back of my head as I was going in and out of consciousness. Frantic, he dialed 911. I can still hear the sound of the sirens, and feel the motion of the high-speed ride that caused the vehicle to forcibly rock back and forth. My first time in an ambulance. When we arrived at the hospital, I stood up from the wheelchair to get into the hospital bed but my body was too weak, and I fell to the floor again. Once in the bed, my body began to shiver violently. Still floating in and out of consciousness, the doctors asked Edwin if I was on drugs. They took my blood and detected that I was unknowingly six weeks pregnant. An ultrasound discovered that it was ectopic and my right fallopian tube burst. I was bleeding internally, and my body was going into shock. They wheeled me in for emergency surgery. My stomach was cut open to remove the tube and embryo. When I woke up, I had tubes coming out of me everywhere. The one in my nose was so irritating. I tried to pull it out instantly without even knowing what I had been through. Finally, I was told, I lost two liters of blood and almost lost my life. I spent four days in the hospital before I was released with a line of staples from my belly button to my pelvis. Thank God, Edwin was home at the time. He saved my life. Eight months later, I was pregnant with our third son.

STAGE FIVE
Roller Coaster Ride

To Have and To Hold

My father, still in Maryland, had suddenly restored his faith in God that Grandma Anna had instilled in all of her children. Surprisingly, he went a step further and began the process of becoming a pastor. This was a man who used to sit on our living room couch with his white papers rolling joints on a Mickey Mouse souvenir tray that he purchased when we went to Disney World. He was living proof that people could change. His number one prayer for his only daughter and her baby daddy was that we stop living in sin. He called constantly sharing his thoughts on how my life should be. One day, Edwin and I finally said, "why not," and we made plans to get hitched. I insisted that we wed in Florida so my whole family could attend stress-free. Aunt Julia, my father's younger sister, was so excited that she offered to plan the entire event. My father paid for everything. My only job was to purchase my wedding dress and show up. However, the last part almost didn't happen.

About a month before the wedding, Edwin sat me down and confessed that he had cheated on me, and that the other woman was pregnant. Anger boiled inside of me. Our relationship wasn't perfect, but I was blindsided by his level of deceit. He admitted his deception because his secret would soon be exposed by his sister who ran into the girl at the mall. I immediately called the wedding off. Edwin pleaded with me not to cancel, as we discussed his infidelity from sunrise to sunset. He swore to me that the relationship with the other woman was over, and all he wanted to do was be a father to his soon to be newborn girl. A daughter. After giving birth to three sons, hearing that he not only cheated on me but was having a little girl was like placing a knife through my heart then twisting it back and forth. The next day, I picked up the phone. The sadness in my voice crept through the receiver as my father listened intensively on the other end. Attempting to console me from miles away, my father patiently listened as I told him the details of Edwin's indiscretion. After a long pause, he replied, "Don't make any rash decisions. Take a couple of days to think about it. Whatever you decide, I will be by your side." So I did exactly what he told me to do, and I thought about it. I thought about all of the money my father had already spent. I thought about all of the time my aunt poured into all of the preparations. I thought about the invitations. I thought about our families. I thought about our friends. I thought about everyone's feelings except my own.

Weeks later, Edwin and I, along with our three sons, Edwin's five sisters, his mother—who just relocated to the United States—his father, and a handful of Edwin's nieces and nephews drove from Hartford, Connecticut to Daytona, Florida in two 12-seat passenger vans. We arrived in Florida a week before the wedding. The moment my foot touched the Florida ground, I turned into a Bridezilla. Everyone brushed off my intense mood swings to pre-wedding jitters. But I knew my attitude stemmed from my uncertainty of whether I was doing the right thing with going through with the wedding.

The familiarity of walking into my grandmother's house brought a sense of calmness over me. Most nights, I would disappear from our hotel room and sit with my aunt and cousins, watching tv in my grandmother's living room. They were unaware of the turmoil in my relationship. However, we all sought out comfort because my grandmother was ill. Her body ravished from diabetes. Days later, she was admitted into hospice. It was an exhausting and emotional time for everyone in my family. On August 20, 1999, our stretch limo pulled up to the beachside park we reserved for our nuptials. It was primetime. My father and I waited for the signal in the backseat. Breathing heavily in my white gown and veil, my father walked me down the sand laced aisle. Edwin stood tall, in his matching attire, awaiting me at the end. As we glared in each other's eyes, repeating the words that would unite us for life, Edwin and I became husband and wife. A few days later, my entire family who just witnessed my wedding was now preparing for a funeral as my grandmother, our matriarch, received her wings.

My wedding day.

Broken Vows

When we arrived back in Connecticut, instead of settling down to marital bliss, things began to get even more complex. I was pregnant again with hopes of giving birth to a baby girl. Excited to get my first ultrasound, I laid down on the table, patiently awaiting the nurse. The friendly technician entered the room and lifted up my gown to expose my flat tummy. I squirmed as she squirted the cold gel on my skin. Although I was used to the routine, the chill of the gel still startled me. Slowly scanning my belly, the talkative technician suddenly became silent. Noticing the look on her face, I asked if everything was okay. She replied that she needed to have a doctor review my ultrasound. As she left the room, I laid there pondering if I was pregnant with twins. Two little girls at once, what a perfect situation to be in. The doctor entered the room and proceeded to conduct his own scan. He whispered to the technician then turned to me and nonchalantly stated, "there is no heartbeat." I began to uncontrollably sob as the news of a miscarriage broke me. All of my dreams of having a little girl were taken away so quickly. A week later, I laid on the hospital table as the doctors performed a D&C.

From day one of the discovery
Of this life inside of me
I gleamed with joy over bringing home
An addition to our family
Thoughts of a girl ran through my head Colors of purple and pink
Names like Janae, Serenca, and Chyna
Cluttered my mind
Hair bows and braids
And little girly games
I thought it would happen this time
With one doctor's visit, everything changed
They said there was no heartbeat
And I was left alone
In a cold doctor's room to weep
People said "it will be ok, you can always try again"
What if again doesn't come around
What will happen then
A child was lost
I was frozen in time
To everyone else, it was just a phase
I should be proud of what I have and move on
Does that mean I shouldn't care
That a part of me is gone
Vanished as if my imagination
Created a bad dream
But a dream it was not
And I will never forget
The day I lost my baby

Even though the miscarriage occurred early in the pregnancy and I had already given birth to three healthy boys, I felt hopeless. My heart was bruised by Edwin's deceit. I held the title of being Edwin's wife, but I saw his baby's mother as my competition.

Subconsciously, I thought if I gave him our own little girl, it would even the playing field. But in reality, I knew it was more than just having babies. He lost my trust. Our life together was moving so fast that we skipped over the part where I healed from his infidelity. In Edwin's mind, the fact that I agreed to get married meant that I had moved on. But all I had really done was temporarily push it out of my mind. It came back, just like everything else left unaddressed. Edwin constantly exclaimed his love for me, and he was a good father to our family. But that wasn't enough. Every time Edwin left the house, I questioned why. Our entire relationship was a roller coaster ride. I could no longer continue to torture myself by speculating about his whereabouts.

My mental anguish began to display itself in the physical form. I stopped having sex with my husband. Just stopped. It wasn't that I didn't find him attractive anymore. My brain was having trouble accepting the fact that the same love he was giving to me, he gave to someone else, so willingly. My reluctance to be intimate with him slowly created a wedge between us, and he soon reverted to his old ways, more drinking and more late nights with the guys. Eventually, he completely stopped pursuing me physically, and it was as if we were living as roommates instead of husband and wife. This went on for months. By Spring, I'd had enough. Less than a year after saying I do, Edwin and I went our separate ways. The revolving door that took hold of my relationship with Edwin had finally closed. We had broken up many times in the past, but this time felt different. It felt final. Nine years had passed since I met Edwin walking down the street. It was nine years of forcing ourselves to be together. For the first time in nine years, I was ready to move on.

Living the Single Life

A group of ladies from my job went out every Friday after work for Happy Hour, and I decided to join them. I pulled into the parking lot of Main-n-Tower, a local bar not far from my house. I hadn't been out solo in years, I nervously sat in the car for a few minutes, checking my hair and barely-there makeup in the rearview mirror. I slowly stepped out of my forest green Toyota Camry, in a tan-colored stretch top and coordinating pants that perfectly snuggled my curves. My silver hoop earrings and heart-shaped pendant necklace glistened in the few remaining rays of the sun. In my peek-a-boo heels, toes painted red, I walked to the entrance with a subtle swerve, when I noticed him.

A tall frame standing by the door watching me. As our bodies got closer, he uttered in a low deep voice, "Hi, what's your name?"

I softly replied, "Sorry, I'm not interested."

He respectfully responded, "No problem, enjoy your night."

Walking past each other, he turned around, his eyes became fixated on my backside as I proceeded to go inside.

As I stepped through the bar doors, the comforting smell of fried fish flowed throughout the air as old-school music streamed from the jukebox. The live DJ wouldn't appear until later in the evening. Making my way to my friends, I felt like the new girl in school all over again as all eyes were on me until I reached my destination at the end of the bar. We all were on our

A-games and free drinks were abundant. Halfway through the night, the tall frame reappeared. Our eyes met and he walked over to formally introduce himself. With his head slighted to the side, still checking me out, he exclaimed, "I'm Dylan." I told him my name, and he offered to buy drinks for my whole crew. We accepted, of course. After a little small talk, he said he didn't want to interrupt my night out with the girls and asked for my phone number so we could continue our conversation another time. I told Dylan that I was fresh out of a relationship and wasn't ready to date. Again, he respectfully responded, "I understand, enjoy your night."

Since I went from high school to motherhood in a blink of an eye. I skipped the partying phase of my life. I wanted to be young again and relive the years that I missed. This was my opportunity to make up for lost time. Technically, I was still Edwin's wife, but things were over between us, I felt it in my soul. To accommodate my new relationship status, I had to buy all new clothes. My work and mommy outfits wouldn't suffice for this phase of my life. Every Friday, when Edwin came to pick up the boys, he was shocked by my transformation. During our years together, I had a closet full of baggy outfits. I had let myself go. What he was now witnessing was the version of me that he had always wanted to see. My nails painted, my hair done, and my curves displayed confidently. For the first time in a long time, I felt a real sense of relief from my responsibilities, and Fish Fry Fridays became my routine. Every time I walked through the bar doors, Dylan was always somewhere, waiting in the distance. For three Fridays straight, he'd come up to me, buy me a drink, and ask to take me out. He was persistent, but not pushy, and always polite. For three Fridays straight, I told him I wasn't ready, but on the fourth Friday, I said yes.

Finding Nino

ylan was seven years my elder, 6'2", and a magnificent dresser. His low-cut fade amplifying his mocha skin. His nickname was Nino because people compared him to Wesley Snipes in New Jack City, but I always called him Dylan. He had three daughters by three different women, who he adored, all the same. With my three sons, we would have been considered the black Brady Bunch. I never met a dude who loved to talk as much as he did. There were many nights that I fell asleep during our pillow talk as I listened as he recanted stories about his life. And if he and Snoop were to ever meet they would instantly connect because Dylan was a cannabis connoisseur. I never smoked.

There was another reason people compared him to Nino. He was a hustler. He did a good job of shielding me from that part of his life, so I don't know how deep he was in the game, but I knew he was a player. In our conversations he talked about his high school track days, and his brothers and sisters, who he admired for their accomplishments. You could hear the sound of regret in his voice when he spoke about the path his own life took. He had a deep love for his mother and wanted her to look at him with pride. The death of his father also took a toll on his emotions leaving him to figure out manhood on his own. After our first date, he wanted to bring me home to meet his mom. At the time, I thought he was crazy and declined the invitation. In retrospect,

I realized that was one of his many ways of showing how much he cared about me without saying the words. I did agree to a double date with his brother and sister-in-law. His family was his everything. Dylan loved going to the movies and deciphering the scenes and plots. We both savored seafood and we relished every bite. He took me to restaurants that were nonexistent in my life prior to meeting him. And this may have been the first time I dated another Sagittarius. His birthday was December 3rd, mine on the 7th.

Growing up with my dad smoking weed normalized it to me, so Dylan's heavy weed use didn't bother me. However, the way he earned his money did. In raising three black sons, I worked hard to keep them far away from that kind of lifestyle. Being Nino would cause constant discontent in our togetherness. He knew how much it agitated me, and he tried to please me by finding regular employment. But the 9 to 5 positions never stuck. Mainly because of the drug tests. He would use the over-the-counter remedies that were supposed to clear your urine, but they didn't work. He had been smoking so long that marijuana became a part of his DNA. And although he tried, we both knew that he wasn't the work-for-someone type, especially not for minimum-wage pennies.

Shortly after meeting Dylan, I learned that he and Edwin knew each other. Like most places, Hartford was a small town, and Dylan and Edwin were former childhood neighbors. I didn't view this as an issue, since I met Dylan after my separation. But in their eyes, it was. Dylan and I dating went against the man code. Throughout my time with Dylan, there was always an underlying cautiousness regarding the circumstances of the two men coming face to face. Thank goodness, it never happened. However, working a full-time job, being a mother to my sons, while trying to figure out how to co-parent with Edwin, and on top of that, build something with Dylan, turned out to be too much for me to handle. I became overwhelmed. In order to breathe, I had to let go of something and Dylan was the only option. I begin to self-sabotage our relationship. I used excuses like "you don't call enough" or "spend enough time with me." I started arguments when there was absolutely nothing to fight about. Consequently, I ended my relationship with Dylan. Not because he cheated on me. Not because he didn't make me feel loved, but simply because I wasn't mentally ready. Our love affair only lasted a season, but it stayed with me for a lifetime.

Let The Church Say Amen

Once I ended things with Dylan, it became a little easier to deal with my strained relationship with Edwin. By November 2001, Edwin and I were on such good terms that I invited him over for Thanksgiving dinner with the kids. For me, the holidays signified family, and Thanksgiving was the epitome of that from my many years of spending it in Florida. After my grandmother's passing, my aunt tried her best to continue our annual family gatherings, but it was never the same. That year I decided, I wanted my children to feel a strong sense of family, and that included their father. Edwin and I still had a deep love and physical attraction for one another. I welcomed him into what was once our home. We bowed our heads to give thanks and Edwin carved the turkey as we sat together in unity. That day became more than just spending the holiday together. Our bond as husband and wife was rekindled. Against all odds, we decided to give our marriage another chance but this time we decided to let God lead us.

For the first time since I was a young girl spending summers in Daytona, I attended church regularly, with my husband and children by my side. Needless to say my father was ecstatic, but it was actually Edwin's idea. A brand-new start, but this time with spiritual guidance. We were one of the youngest married couples there. There was a sense that the church felt an obligation to counsel us. We went to Sunday school and bible study. We decided to get our two older boys baptized. For children to be baptized, they had to be able to read, so our third son was too young. I was asked to join the choir, but I inherited the singing voice of my late grandmother and knew it would be disastrous. Then I was asked to participate as an usher. I'm not sure how I got out of that one. Edwin was offered to commit to a weekly men's gathering, which he attended a few times.

At home, we limited television watching in exchange for board games and books. Quality family time was the priority. In November of 2002, we became a family of six after I gave birth to our fourth son. I requested a four-month maternity leave from work, the longest amount of time I have ever taken off since I began working at the age of sixteen. During my interim as a stay-at-home mom, I kept busy with our sons and the household chores, and I adapted to it well. However, our presence in the church declined. It began months earlier, toward the end of my pregnancy. My swollen feet, back pains, and lack of sleep made it easy for me to resist early Sunday morning excursions. After I gave birth, I needed time to heal. Then I thought the baby was too young to bring around such a large congregation. Also, it was during the winter months and it was daunting to bring a newborn outside in the cold air. One excuse led to another, and we stopped going to church altogether. Once the weekly rhythm of attending service was interrupted, I didn't want to go at all. Before having our fourth son, we were so involved in the church that we morphed into people that I no longer recognized. But that was the whole point of going to church in the first place, right? To do things differently to make our relationship work. The sudden change was something I wasn't accustomed to, and I felt like a fraud in the House of the Lord. My heart wanted a deeper relationship with God, but my mind was not ready for the transformation. It felt as if Edwin and I were forcing ourselves to live a *Leave It to Beaver* lifestyle when neither of our true behaviors were anything close to that. The religious foundation we were building was the glue binding us together. Once we removed that bond, our relationship began to crumble.

What happened next was inevitable. Edwin revived his habit of hanging out late with his friends as primary entertainment, while I slowly began to lose trust again. Months passed and our connection to one another faded. I never fully regained the trust I had with him when we first met, and he was wavering between being a devoted husband and fighting the female temptations that surrounded him every day. The happiness we once shared had fallen through the cracks so deep that there was no coming back. Although pain still lingered in my heart from his previous infidelity, the truth was that we were growing in two different directions. I didn't want to talk about our problems anymore. I didn't want to confide in anyone. I didn't want to try to go to counseling to work things out. We were husband and wife, but we were not meant to be together forever. Right before my youngest son turned two, my relationship with Edwin was through. This time it was for good.

STAGE SIX
Revealing Me

Raising Boys to Men

B ecoming a mother made me realize that one of the most rewarding experiences in your life can also be one of the most challenging ones. Like Tupac said, "for a woman, it ain't easy tryna raise a man." Now multiply that times four. There's no handbook to this parenting thing. As young boys, my time was spent bringing my sons to different sporting events. They played basketball, baseball, and football. Every summer was filled with camp from beginning to end. From day one, my strategy was to keep them busy. The more engrossed they were with positive activities, the fewer chances there were for them to get into trouble, or so I thought. It was easy when they were young because every move they made was under my control. They wanted to go to the park, they needed a ride. They had to ask mommy. They wanted to buy candy from the store, they needed money. They had to ask mommy. They wanted to go over to a friend's house to play. That friend's mother would tell my kids to ask your mother if it was ok. Easy, right? However, with each year that passed, the more independent my sons became, my control narrowed. My oldest son set the blueprint for what was to come.

It always starts with high school, the teenage years, hanging out with the wrong crowds. Of course, I blamed the other kids. Yet, deep in my heart, I knew I was wrong, considering Hudson, my oldest son, was never a follower. He was a fighter, never afraid to stand his ground. He knew from early on it was the only way for him to gain respect. He had a heart of gold with a street kid mentality. The combination of his mother and father in one seed. He was the firstborn, destined to lead, a warrior on the basketball court, and a master pitcher on the baseball field. Athletics came natural for him. He prospered in any sport he played. His schoolwork, on the other hand, lagged. It was hard to keep him on track. The phone calls from school were constant, and none of them were good. His lack of respect for his teachers made him a staple in the detention room. Now, add the distraction of girls into the mix, and all hope seemed lost. In my frustration, his father stepped up and decided to take him in full time. I hesitated at first, then thought, why not, it worked in *Boyz n the Hood*. But my life wasn't a screenplay. The phone calls from school persisted, and I started to have doubts about my decision. In my mind, things were getting worse, but now I had absolutely no control. Edwin was upset when I showed up at his house and told my son to pack. He was coming back home to live with me, facing a new set of boundaries. At fifteen I enrolled him in the Summer Youth Employment Program, and he started earning his own money. He actually worked at his high school, following the janitor's rules, cleaning the floors, and emptying the trash, learning the rewards of hard work set him on a new path.

Meanwhile, son number two was the opposite in school. Edison was the teacher's pet, praised by everyone he knew. His report cards and tests were all covered with A's. A competitive kid, basketball, and baseball were his specialties. Until he picked up a football in his early teens and became the shortest quarterback on his high school team. He even gave track a try, but just for one season. He was a little bit of a jokester. One look at him, he resembled his mama through and through. His brown eyes were an exact replica of mine. I often wondered how brothers, only two and a half years part, could be so opposite. Until one day, while at work, I received a call from the afterschool program my children were enrolled in. They said my sons got into a fight. When I arrived both Edison and Hudson were sitting in the office. The administrator of the program told me a group of boys was picking on Edison. At the time, Hudson was shooting hoops on the basketball court when someone alerted him that his younger brother was about to get jumped. The administrator continued the story by telling me that Hudson ran over and fought all the boys. And that's when I knew. Edison's ride was a little easier because he didn't have to go through the hood ritual of proving his toughness. Everyone knew that if you messed with Edison, you would have a problem with Hudson. He was his brother's keeper.

And when I thought brothers couldn't be any more different, my third son Branson proved me wrong. From day one, he reminded me of my brother Titus. A hard exterior with a quiet soul. He would sit in the house for hours, never saying a word. Often teased by his siblings, being the youngest of the three, his fights were inside the house, not on the streets. Hudson felt that since Branson was so much younger he wouldn't be around to protect him as he did with Edison, so he had to strengthen him up. But Hudson's legacy lasted beyond his years in school and just being his brother was enough. Branson took the toughness he was taught and applied it to sports. As soon as his cleats touched the football field, my quiet son transformed into a beast. From a young kid into his late teens, playing football was his only dream. It increased his confidence, trained him in leadership and teamwork, and taught him to be ambitious. Skills that we all need.

For my youngest son, Jackson, I'm patiently waiting to see who he will be. The baby of the bunch. He was raised with a gentle touch. I didn't assign household chores to him like I did my older three. Cleaning his room and getting good grades in school was

My four sons.

his only requirement. I didn't purposely set out to treat him differently. A part of me was burned out, and as I got older I realized that my past parenting methods did not always work out. He played sports, just like his siblings but his passion wasn't the same. His Xbox kept calling his name. The video games, apps, and tablets, his generation was more focused on the new electronic gadgets. Making him a prisoner to his room. But there is one thing he loves, animals, something he inherited from his father. From big cats, reptiles, birds, and aquatic creatures, he watches all the animal shows on tv with thoughts of one day working in a zoo. I'm hoping he also watched the lessons learned from his older brothers, to assist him down the right path when he enters adulthood.

The storms never quite settle when you are raising four sons. Once you douse out one fire, another flame slowly burns somewhere in the background. There were times that I struggled balancing life as a single mother, and I felt like a failure. I yelled at them when they needed to be nurtured. Instead of listening to their concerns, I scolded them for speaking out of turn, not knowing if I was doing more harm or making them strong. But I knew my heart was big enough, and I knew my love was strong enough, to defend all of my choices. And I was encouraged because I knew there was a reason God gave me four little angels to keep. Raising boys to men was my destiny.

The first blessing came at the age of eighteen.
In one flash you appeared and it seemed to be a dream.
Now God has given me four angels to keep.
And I kneel down and thank Him every night before I sleep.
Your brown eyes are so precious. Your innocence is so unique.
From infant, to toddler to young men. It's amazing to me.
I watch you grow and pray that the world treats you fair.
I hope the hard lessons are fair and few and are easy to repair.
My four little angels, I thank you for the lessons I learned from you.
That just a touch or caring words can heal all wounds.

On My Own

In 2004, my "I don't need a man" mode was in full swing when I decided to purchase my first home all by myself. Owning a home was something Edwin and I discussed for years. We drove down streets looking at For Sale signs, knowing one day it would be us popping on the Sold sticker. It never happened, but I refused to let my dream die just because my marriage did. My first house was a tan, three-bedroom, two-bathroom Cape Cod-style with a huge fenced-in backyard, lined with trees. The front walkway was encrusted with bushes that lead straight to the burgundy door. In the fall, the thousands of leaves covering the yard became my nemesis but it was all worth it. For the first time in my adult life, I wasn't living under the order of a man. Furniture choice, mine. Paint color, mine. Accessories, mine. My opinion was the only one that mattered.

This method of living was also applied to my luscious, non-committal dating life. I kissed every frog that leaped in my direction, older men, younger men, working nine-to-five guys, street guys, I live in my grandmother's basement dudes, baby-mama drama dudes, and I even considered taking a dip in the vanilla pond after a white guy complimented me while we were waiting in line at CVS. But my independent woman celebration came to an end when I was so caught up in living carefree that I neglected some of my monetary responsibilities. My finances were a mess. I had no clue what it meant to own a home. Living in rental properties all of my adult life created a sense of ignorance. I had always had the comfort of dialing a phone number when something wasn't working right. Homeownership is not for the weak, especially if you are doing it solo. The upkeep of the vast backyard alone was difficult to maintain. Never mind the time when the water heater sprung a leak when the basement flooded because the roots from the enormous oak tree out front decided to occupy my pipes, or the expense of filling the oil tank for the long, bitterly cold winters in New England.

Cosmetically, I envisioned remodeling the kitchen, tearing down the lower-level half-wall to create fluidity, and finishing the extra room in the basement that had exposed studs and a concrete floor. None of it occurred. Every single cent this independent chick made went toward bills. As years passed, there was more money floating out of my pockets than landing in them. I was house poor. I considered getting a second job, but then what would that mean for my kids? I enjoyed being that parent screaming their names from the stands at all of their games. Making sure they ate breakfast before school and rushing home from work to put dinner on the table. A second job would have taken all that away. After six years of owning property, I made the sacrifice to let go of something my wallet could no longer hold on to, my first home.

Back to Reality

Finding myself living in a two-bedroom apartment with my four sons after owning a home was a humiliating experience. I failed, and everyone knew it. I relinquished the master bedroom to my children, it was large. It housed a bunk bed with a twin-size mattress on top and a full-size mattress on the bottom. I also managed to fit a separate full-size bed in the opposite corner of the room. My oldest son had graduated from high school by this time, and he was partially living with his girlfriend. But on nights when things weren't going right with them, which happened often, he stayed on my couch. The huge living adjustment was compensated by the financial turmoil that was lifted from me physically and emotionally. It was a decent apartment complex. Amenities included a pool, small gym area, tennis court, and laundry facilities on every floor. No more trotting down to a cold, damp basement to wash clothes. There were six, three-story brick buildings in total. When you entered through the gates it felt like you were in your own little community. Grocery stores were within walking distance, although I always drove. There was also a sense of ease with the release of responsibility of having to fix things. Rent, electricity, and cable were my only bills, and all within my financial grasp. Although the windows were poorly insulated, and heat and air conditioning left a hefty mark on the electric bill. I began telling myself that homeownership wasn't for me. It was too hard, too much work. But the lies I told myself didn't rest well in my soul. I knew I deserved more.

I was at a crossroads at work. Throughout the years, I had gone from one job to the next searching for the right fit. I worked as a clerical assistant, human resources assistant, and executive assistant. No matter the position, like clockwork, I felt stagnant after a few years of employment. My reasons for leaving one job for the next would always blur together. I finally recognized the work pattern I self-created, and I decided to change it. I enrolled in an accelerated degree program at Albertus Magnus College to obtain a bachelor's degree in business. It had been twenty years since I graduated from high school when I found myself back inside a classroom. I decided to go back while raising my sons and working a full-time job. It was almost comical. I hated school as a child, but deep down I knew it was exactly what I needed.

With each academic project, I seized an opportunity to select a black woman for my topic. I researched Bessie Coleman, Josephine Baker, Mary McLeod Bethune, and Madam C. J. Walker, to name a few. All clear reminders of ancestral strength and perseverance. Those remarkable women possessed the passion to pursue their goals despite the incredible social and economic barriers set against them. So, there was no excuse for me to sit back and not go after mine. I enrolled in college so I could obtain a better job and further provide for my sons. In turn, what I received was far greater, a new level of confidence that allowed me to tackle all obstacles.

I contacted a mortgage company to establish the steps I needed to take in order to qualify for a loan. It took me two years to repair my credit, and in 2016 I purchased another home. I made sure not to buy something at the top of my price range, a lesson I learned from owning my previous home. This time it was a pale-yellow ranch, nestled in a cul-de-sac in East Hartford. It was one thousand square feet with a full finished basement. My children were getting older, and it was the perfect size to manage for the empty-nester stage of my life. Being move-in ready was a plus. I didn't even have to paint. Although, Branson insisted on painting his room a deep dark blue. I counted the trees outside, there were three. I thought that would limit the exterior upkeep. I was wrong. The leaves from my neighbors' trees blew into my yard. Thank goodness for my four sons.

Two years later, my sons stood in the audience as they watched me strut across the stage to accept my college degree. I was checking the box next to all of my goals and accomplishments. I walked away from school with so many business ideas swirling in my brain. I attempted one, a dating website specializing in single moms. That fell through due to the amount of money required to advertise and compete with the big leagues. Then there was my food truck idea. Not the average on-the-go meals, but I can't share what it is because it still may be a possibility. I was trying my best to come up with a way to create generational wealth, so my children and the children after them wouldn't have to weigh getting a second job versus spending time with their kids. But the one thing that I didn't plan and what set my soul free, was the one thing I kept hidden. It was my poetry.

My college graduation.

The Awakening

As a young girl, I first fell in love with poetry while flipping through the pages of my father's Jet magazines. Picture this little ponytailed girl, running to the mailbox to grab the weekly treat. I would pass the self-help articles and the melanin *Beauty of the Week*, all the way in the back, would be a few poems that I would always read. The flow, style, and story would always capture me. I was a fan. I never imagined it as something I could do. Until one day in the midst of anger, I picked up a pen and paper and the words flew out of me, too. It was during my marriage. Pissed, for whatever reason, all of my emotions poured out of me, and I immediately felt a sense of relief. Poetry became my therapy. I wrote about everything. From men to children. From love to pain. I jotted down word after, word. It allowed me to breathe again. But it was my secret. Only for my eyes. I wasn't ready to reveal all of myself until one day I realized that sharing my passion would set me free.

Despite writing since I was in my twenties, I didn't have the courage to publish my first poetry book until much later in my life. Looking back, I wish I had done it sooner. I am always amazed when a person recognizes what they want to be at a young age. For example, when my oldest son was a teenager he wanted to design sneakers. I stealthily used the equipment at work and printed a pile of blank shoe outlines so he could draw his designs. He used colored pencils and made tons of patterns.

Admiring his creativity, I suggested fashion school so he could live out his dream. Well, he lost interest after a few months and his designs became lost in space.

When my third son decided he wanted to be an artist after taking a class in high school, I brought an assortment of paint colors, brushes, canvas boards, and even an easel so he could easily set up in his room. I imagined covering the empty walls of my house with his magnificent creations. He completed one painting. The supplies now live in the back of his closet.

When my second son decided that he wanted to be a teacher, I encouraged him to figure out which age group he preferred to help him decipher whether to pursue a degree in elementary or secondary education. He was accepted to college and majored in secondary education with a concentration in English. By his junior year in college, he scored a mini-apartment on campus and roomed with five other students. The distractions were enormous. He is a middle school paraprofessional now, still working on earning his degree.

At the age of sixteen my youngest son informed me that he wanted to work with animals for a living. I thought the best way for him to gain experience with other animals besides playing fetch with our pet dogs, was for him to volunteer at an animal shelter. I contacted everyone in our area and was told that he needed to be eighteen years of age to volunteer.

When my children shared their dreams with me, I saw the spark in their eyes that was missing from mine when I was a child. I felt an urge to assist them in their journey whether it was a momentary vision or a lifelong goal.

For years, when it came to my own dreams, that urge was missing. I thought my only purpose was to provide for my children, work a job that would supply enough money to put food on their plates, clothes on their backs, and a roof over their heads. My life was on continual repeat, and I became robotic with daily routines. Up at 6 a.m. Get kids ready for school. Work from 9 to 5. Cook dinner. Check homework. In bed by 10 pm. As long as I was doing this, I thought I was fulfilling my purpose. The truth was I couldn't see the bigger plan God had for me. That this self-proclaimed introvert had a voice that people wanted to hear. I spent years blocking my gift all because of fear. Afraid that no one cared about this little black girl from Jersey. I didn't know who I was. I didn't know that we all had a choice. I didn't know that every single one of us had value. I didn't know until my awakening occurred. It wasn't a hugely powerful moment that overcame me. One day I woke up and realized I was feeding everyone else's goals and desires while leaving mine to starve. I finally decided that I was worthy of happiness, and my dreams deserved my energy. Some of my past experiences delayed me, but they didn't defeat me. I embraced my journey, the good and the bad. Finally, I put myself first and pursued my purpose.

My first poetry book was the first step. Appropriately titled, *The Awakening Book of Poems*. Like my poetry, I kept my book a secret until it was ready to be released. Only my children knew. The book was just for me, so no marketing plan was made. But when I finally announced it, I was surprised at the amount of support it received. A clear indication that I found my path. Hiding behind the invisible walls of social media, I began promoting my book. Then I built up the courage to sign up for events. Jazz, Blues, Folk, Arts and Crafts, were a variety of festivals on my list. My vendor table became a success. As people approached me, they picked up my book with a glimmer in their eyes. Encouraged by my work, some had their own hopes of writing. They asked all sorts of questions about the cover, my process, and my style. I discovered in my journey of finding myself, I was an influencer as well. That my voice, that I thought was so small, actually spoke volumes, and impacted others. That little lost Jersey girl will always be a part of me, but now instead of shying away in a corner, I stand tall as a proud author and confess my life stories. God willing, I still have a lot of life to live. I hope that one day my grandchildren look at me with the same admiration as I did with Grandma Anna. Going forward, the plan is to keep writing, keep pushing, and dream bigger. I kneel down every day and pray for good health, monetary wealth, and true love. I hope that those who are lost, as I was, will also find their way. My goal is to one day return to that place that holds all my fond family memories. Not as a visitor, instead as a resident. Picture me leaving a trail of footprints on a sandy Florida beach, my toes barely visible through the water as I'm lounging in my seat. Sporting a white two-piece bathing suit and a matching cover-up because I'm still shy. Big sunglasses covering my eyes. The side table next to my chair holds my glass of wine, slow sipping each time. With my laptop on my thighs, my fingers typing left to right, thinking of all the things life has to teach us, going from brick buildings to beaches. Living my best life.

Look in the mirror and what do I see? A beautiful Nubian Queen. But my thinking hasn't always been so clear. There was a time in my life when I held many fears. Fear of self, insecure about who I was. This brown-skinned girl thought the lighter girls had it all. Soft hair, small features, and all the guys listening. I thought my curves were the only way to get their attention. Motherless daughter, wandering through life with no womanly figure. Teenage mother, destined to become a statistic. Raised by a single dad, this young girl had a model of strength. A strength that turned into belief. Belief in my abilities made me embrace my reality and lead with stability. I looked in the mirror and glimpsed past the physical image. And saw the spirit of my father, the heart of my children, and the courage of my ancestors. For the first time, I saw me.

About the Author

Author Sharika K. Forde has a passion for creative expression. In 2017, she pushed her fear aside and published her first poetry book. She has since published a memoir, two poetry books, and a collection of children's books, all inspired by life lessons. Beginning each day with a prayer for good health, monetary wealth, and true love, she strives to live a life of fulfillment through her passion for writing.

Other Books by the Author:

Poetry Books:
The Awakening Poems Vol 1; Bare Emotions of Love, Growth, & Self-Worth
The Awakening Poems Vol 2; I Dream in Color

Children's Books:
Grandma's Lil' King
Grandpa's Lil' Queen
Grandma's Lil' King Plays T-Ball
Grandma's Lil' Math King
The Moon, The Stars, and Fast Cars